UPSIDE-DOWN TOWN

TOWN

by

F. Emerson Andrews

Illustrated by Louis Slobodkin

LITTLE, BROWN AND COMPANY

Boston · Toronto

For

FELICITY RUSSELL

who was the first to visit

UPSIDE-DOWN TOWN

with me

*Published simultaneously in Canada
by Little, Brown & Company (Canada) Limited*

PRINTED IN THE UNITED STATES OF AMERICA

Contents

1. Upside-Down Town

FOR hours and hours Rickie and Anne rode in the train with red coaches on the way to Grandfather's. Rickie let Anne, who was smaller, sit at the window, but he could see out, too. There wasn't much to see except fields, and now and then a house, a tall windmill, and a few scrawny trees.

The nice, even clickety-click changed to a screech, and the train stopped with a bump. They saw the Conductor in his blue coat outside, walking very fast toward the head of the train. Rickie leaned against the window, but all he could see was that they were stopped near a river.

Soon the Conductor came back, a whistle blew, the train gave a bump and started moving.

"We're going backward," said Anne.

"So we are," said Rickie, seeing the trees go by in the wrong direction. "I don't believe this is a good way to get to Grandfather's."

The train went backward for quite a long time, and then it began to slow down. They were getting into a town. Rickie crowded to the window. Was this Lancaster where Grandfather would meet them?

They were backing into a station. The sign didn't look like LANCASTER. It looked like this:

"Rickie, can you read that?" asked Anne.

"No, it must be in some other language."

Just then the Conductor in his blue coat with the big brass buttons opened the door and called out:

"Upside-Down Town! All passengers out!"

"I still can't make out that sign," said Rickie.

"Silly! Didn't you hear the Conductor? We're in Upside-Down Town. You have to twist your head around, and then you can read it plain. It's printed upside down because we're in Upside-Down Town!"

The other passengers all left, but Daddy had told Rickie and Anne to stay right in their seats until they got to Lancaster. So they sat and waited. Only nothing happened. After a while the Conductor came in again, and looked surprised.

"Are you still here? All passengers must get out."

"My Daddy said to stay until we reach Grandfather's in Lancaster," said Rickie.

"Oh, I see," said the Conductor, and he had a nice, big, friendly smile. "But there's been trouble on the Main Line. A bridge fell down. So we had to back up into Upside-Down Town, and we must wait here until they get the bridge repaired. But the Railroad will take care of you, and notify your grandfather so he won't worry."

"How long will it be?" asked Anne.

"I don't know. At least until sometime tomorrow. But it's the Railroad's fault, so you won't have to pay anything. Come, and I'll take you over to the Hotel where all the passengers are staying."

"Oh, goody!" said Rickie. "I stayed in a hotel once with Daddy, and it was lots of fun."

The Conductor helped them down the high steps of the car.

"The Hotel is over this way," said the Conductor, and they started walking.

"We don't usually go into Upside-Down Town," said the Conductor. "In the first place, they have a rule that trains have to run into it backward, and things are so different here we always get mixed up. Look at those houses, for instance."

They were just passing a house that looked a good bit like the one-story ranch houses Rickie and Anne saw in new sections of their own town. But this house seemed to face inward instead of toward the street, and a short ramp ran from the street up to the roof. Just at this moment a man drove a car up onto the roof, parked it, opened a trapdoor, and went down inside.

"My goodness," said Rickie. "Do they always keep cars on the roof instead of in a basement garage?"

"They say it's sensible," said the Conductor. "It makes the cars easier to start on cold days, and the flat roofs are just as good for helicopters. Five or six of the Upside-Down Town people have helicopters now, and they say everybody may have one soon."

"It's a funny-looking car, too," said Anne. "It doesn't seem to have any hood."

"Its a Topsy," said the Conductor. "It's made by the Topsy-Turvy Company, Upside-Down Town's big-

gest industry. It just looks funny because it has the engine in the back. They say that's much more sensible. This way the driver can see better where he is going because he is almost there already, and the engine is right over the wheels it has to push."

After walking about three blocks from the station they came out on a large public square. The Conductor pointed to a long, low building across the Square.

"That's the Hotel where they are expecting you," he said. "I have to leave you now, and send a lot of telegrams."

2. Hotel

"WHAT does the sign say?" asked Anne.

"It says HOTEL, only it's upside down," said Rickie, who was getting used to the ways of Upside-Down Town. "This is going to be fun. We'll be in a room way high up and have to use an elevator. Have you been in an elevator, Anne?"

"Of course," said Anne. "To get to Daddy's office. But we can't be in a room very high up. See, the Hotel is only two stories."

"So it is," said Rickie. "I don't see how this can be a real hotel, then. They're supposed to be big and tall."

They went in the door and looked around. In the center of the room was a play pen, and inside it on a cushion sat an old man with a long white beard. Three books were piled neatly beside him, but just now he was playing with the beads on a counting frame. He paid no attention to them. At the far end of the room was the Hotel desk, and a boy just a little older than Rickie perched on a stool behind it.

Rickie walked up to him a bit doubtfully, holding Anne by the hand.

"Are you in charge here?"

"Yes," said the boy in a squeaky voice. "And we are expecting you. Since it is the Railroad's fault you are delayed, they will pay everything."

"But — but," said Anne, "how is it you are doing the work and the old man there is sitting down and playing and reading?"

"Just call me Charlie," said the clerk. "And now I'll explain. See how happy that man is?"

Anne and Rickie saw that the old man was now reading a book. When he stopped reading to chuckle, as he did every now and then, he used his long beard as a page marker. It was evidently a very funny book.

"You see," said Charlie the clerk, "in Upside-Down Town the children do all the work, and the old folks play. A very sensible arrangement it is, too. That old man used to run this Hotel, and he got very tired of it after working forty years. He deserves a rest, and now he just plays and reads. Besides, that lets me run the Hotel, which is great fun. What's your name?"

"I'm Rickie."

"Well, Rickie, wouldn't you like to sit up here and ring bells for bell boys and run a hotel?"

"I sure would!" said Rickie.

"Or be a policeman like my brother, or bake pies like my sister, or maybe even be allowed to run the washing machine?"

"That would be fun!" said Anne.

"You see, it's much better for us children to do the work while it's still new and fun, and for the old people, who are maybe a little tired anyway, to rest and play."

"That's certainly right," said Rickie. "I'm beginning to like Upside-Down Town."

"You'll get along fine here," said Charlie, "if you only remember that everything is backward."

"We'll try," said Anne and Rickie together.

"All right. Now before I send you to your rooms, you'd better go to the Restaurant and have something to eat."

"Good," said Rickie. "I'm practically always hungry."

16

3. From Dessert to Soup

RICKIE looked around until he saw a long sign that might spell "Restaurant" upside down. They entered the room. Sure enough, it was full of tables and chairs, and some of the other people from the train were already eating.

A little girl about Anne's age came up to them.

"Are you the waitress?" asked Anne.

"Yes," said the girl. "My name is Felicity; call me Flickie, for short."

"Do you have to wait on table?"

"Of course not!" said Flickie. "I do it because it is such fun. And it's most fun when we can serve people who don't know about Upside-Down Town food."

"Is it any different?" Anne asked.

"In some ways," said the girl. "You'll find out."

"Well, I'm hungry," said Rickie, "so the sooner we find out the better. Could we have our suppers now?"

"Yes. Is there anything special you want?"

"I'll take all the specials you have," decided Anne. "I'm hungry."

"So will I," agreed Rickie, "but twice as much of each."

"All right," said Flickie. "Now I'll bring you our very special dessert."

"Dessert?" protested Rickie. "But we want the full meal. We'll even eat soup."

"You will get it," promised Flickie, "but in Upside-Down Town of course you eat the dessert first. Besides, this gives us time to cook the hot things."

In a moment Flickie was back, carrying on a big tray two pieces of what looked like lemon cake with white icing on top. She put a piece before each of them.

"It's a very special dessert tonight," she said.

Rickie tasted his cake. It was a little bitey on the tongue, as lemon should be; the white icing on top was sweet and very good.

"It's fine," he said, "but I don't see what's different about it. Mother gives us cake like this all the time."

"You wouldn't get cake like this anywhere else,"

said Flickie. "You see, it's really upside-down cake served right side up."

When they knew what it really was, the cake did taste a little extra good.

Next she asked them what meat they would like.

"Could I have a lamb chop?" asked Anne.

"In Upside-Down Town," said Flickie, "we couldn't give you a lamb chop. We'll give you chopped lamb."

So she did. It came in on a big plate, with string beans and a potato on the side and a piece of toast on top of the meat.

"Just what I thought would happen!" boasted Rickie. "In most places they put your meat on the toast; here they serve it the other way round. Only I do wish she had buttered my toast."

Anne burst out laughing.

"Look at your fingers, smarty!"

His fingers were all smeared with rich, yellow butter. Of course the toast had been buttered on the bottom side.

As the last course Flickie brought on two large bowls, each about half full of soup. She stirred each bowl before she set it down.

"You keep stirring it, too," she said. "It only tastes good if it's turned round and round. It's turn-turtle soup."

After they finished their turn-turtle soup, they thanked Flickie for the good meal and decided to ask for their room and go right to bed. They were a little tired from so exciting a day.

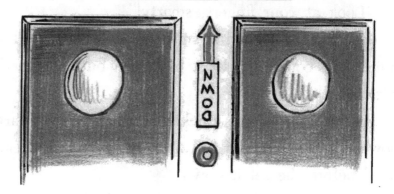

4. Room 501

RICKIE and Anne went back to the Hotel desk, where Charlie was waiting for them with their room key.

"You are on the fifth floor," he said. "I'm giving you a nice double room, Room Five Hundred and One."

"Fifth floor!" said Rickie. "But we looked, and this Hotel is only two stories high."

"High," agreed Charlie. "But we have eight cellar floors. You're in the fifth, going down."

"You mean we have to live in the cellar?" protested Anne. "That's where you put all your guests?"

"What could be more sensible?" said Charlie. "If you build a hotel high, there's always danger of its blowing over or falling down. Besides, the traffic outside makes the rooms noisy, and the light disturbs the guests. So we put them down cellar, where it's cool and safe and pleasant. Of course, every room is air-conditioned."

"You make it sound fine," said Rickie. "But what do you put on the second floor? I saw you had one."

"That's for the coal and other supplies," explained Charlie the clerk. "We just open a chute with the right label — COAL, or BREAD, or SHEETS — and the supplies we need come tumbling down. That way nobody has to carry anything."

"What a clever idea!" said Rickie. "Well, we're a little tired now. We'll take our bags to our room. Where is the elevator?"

"The Delevator is over there," said Charlie. "It doesn't elevate, it goes down."

The Delevator let them off at the fifth basement. Here they found three corridors, one going to the right, one to the left, and one straight ahead. They saw arrows, with room numbers. But two of the arrows both pointed to Room 501, down different corridors.

"It's lucky there are two of us," said Rickie, "so we can try both at once."

So Rickie took the right-hand corridor, and Anne the one straight front. Anne walked the whole length

of her corridor, and couldn't see any Room 501. When she got back to the Delevator, there was Rickie.

"I walked the whole way down my corridor," said Rickie, "and there was no Room Five Hundred and One. It must be down yours."

"It isn't," said Anne.

"Must be!" insisted Rickie.

Anne looked ready to cry. Then she laughed instead.

"We're so silly!" she said. "Of course in Upside-Down Town, to get to a place you go where the arrows don't point."

So they went down the hall where no arrow pointed to Room 501, and it was the very first door.

It was a lovely room, with twin beds. They were very tired, so they both got into their pajamas and brushed their teeth.

"How shall we ever know when to get up?" asked Anne. "It's dark down here."

Rickie remembered how his father in a hotel had picked up the telephone and asked the clerk to call him at seven o'clock. So he picked up the phone and did that too. Then, very pleased with himself, he switched off the light and started to climb into bed.

Only he couldn't. The covers were tucked in tight.

"Rickie," said Anne's voice in the darkness, "I can't seem to get into this bed at all."

"I know," said Rickie. "You get in at the bottom and sleep upside down."

So they did. In a minute more they were both sound asleep.

5. The Doctor

DING-A-LING!

Rickie and Anne both woke up. Rickie switched on the light, which of course was at the foot of the bed. The telephone was ringing. He took up the receiver.

"Hello?"

"Seven o'clock," said a voice that sounded like Charlie's. "Don't you want to see something of Upside-Down Town?"

"Oh, all right," said Rickie, still a little sleepy. "We'll get dressed right away, and come down — I mean, up!"

They dressed, and had a good breakfast, beginning with eggs fried sunny side down, and then cereal, and finally orange juice. Then they went out into the Hotel lobby, where Charlie the clerk was waiting for them.

27

"It will be a while until your train is ready. Don't you want to go shopping, maybe, or see a ball game?"

"Shopping!" said Anne.

"I want to see a ball game," said Rickie.

"You will have time for both, but you'd better see the ball game first. The Bigger League plays its games early in the morning, when it's cool and the players are fresh."

"The Bigger League?" asked Rickie. "What's that?"

"You have to be a grandfather to play," explained Charlie. "The rules are a little different, too. I wish I could take time off to show you."

Just then the old man from the play pen stepped up.

"I'm Mr. Drake," he said. "I'm a little too old to play ball, so they made me the bat boy. My team isn't playing today, so I'll be glad to take you and explain the game."

They had just started for the ball park with Mr. Drake when Anne stopped and put her hand on her tummy.

"I don't feel so good," she said. "Maybe it's something I ate."

"That's too bad," said Mr. Drake. "Maybe you're not used to upside-down cake served right side up.

People do get upset here because things are different. We'll see a doctor, and have you fixed in a jiffy."

"Oh, dear," said Anne. "Now Rickie will miss the ball game he wants so much to see."

"Not at all. Look, right across the street is the doctors' waiting room."

"Of course we must go," said Rickie. "But Mother has taken us to doctors' waiting rooms, and it's hours until they get around to seeing you."

"You must have misunderstood me," said Mr. Drake.

"In Upside-Down Town we don't have patients' waiting rooms; this is a doctors' waiting room, where the doctors wait for patients."

Mr. Drake held the door for them. They were suddenly in a large room, with about a dozen desks ranged around it, and behind each desk was a doctor dressed in white. The doctors were reading old magazines the patients had left behind.

Anne noticed a little sign on each desk. The first one read:

> DR. PATCHIT
> Sprains
> Broken Bones

The next sign read:

> DR. KAUFMAN
> Colds and Hots
> Sneezes

The third sign read:

> DR. AKERS
> Tummy Aches
> Gastronomic Disorders

Anne went right up to Dr. Akers.

"Excuse me, but I've got a tummy ache. Could you do something for me?"

"Of course," said Dr. Akers. "Come with me. Your brother can come along."

Anne and Rickie followed the doctor along a short corridor into a little room with a desk, two visitors' chairs, and a funny jointed thing that straightened out into a bed at a touch of a lever.

"Stick out your tongue," said Dr. Akers.

He looked at it a moment, and then opened the door of a small refrigerator and pulled out a dish with a nice brown ball in it that looked like ice cream. He gave Anne a spoon, and pulled out his watch.

"One, two, three . . . Eat!"

It was chocolate ice cream.

"This is a pleasanter way to take a temperature than by sticking a gaggy thermometer under a person's tongue," he explained. "You see, ice cream melts faster in the mouth of a person with a high fever, so a sick person gets done sooner."

While Anne was enjoying having her temperature taken, Rickie thought he had better speak up.

"Dr. Akers, we ought to tell you right away that we were going to Grandfather's, and got stuck in Upside-

Down Town by accident. We haven't any money. But I'm sure if you make out a bill, Father will pay you when we get back home."

"Pay?" said Dr. Akers. "In Upside-Down Town doctors get paid only for keeping people well. But as soon as our patients get sick, of course they stop paying us. Even if it wasn't our fault they got sick, still they can't work until we get them well again, so how could they pay? We think this is a much more sensible arrangement."

Just at this moment Anne finished the last spoonful of chocolate ice cream. Dr. Akers looked quickly at his wrist watch.

"You ate that rather slowly," he reported. "Three minutes and forty-one seconds. So you have almost no fever. All that's wrong with you is eating a bit too much when you were excited. And maybe you're not used to having your meals backwards. I'll give you a pill that will fix you right up."

He went over to a shelf and took down a big glass bottle full of pink pills. He took one out, and put a bit of water in a glass.

"Here, swallow this, and then wash it down."

Anne made a face.

"I hate pills."

"Try this one," said Dr. Akers, "and you might be surprised."

Anne put the pink pill in her mouth, tasted it a second, and then a smile spread all over her face. She rolled the pill around on her tongue, and only after a long while, when it was nearly gone, did she drink the rest of it down.

"Why, that's better than the best candy! I never tasted anything so nice!"

"Of course," said Dr. Akers. "Since pills are to make people well, we make them as tasty as possible so people will be sure to take them."

"If I lived in Upside-Down Town," said Anne, "I'd be sick all the time, so I could have a pill every day."

"No, you wouldn't," said Dr. Akers. "You see, if the first pill doesn't get you well, we have to change the dose. And since we put all of our very best tastes in the first pill, the next ones aren't quite so good, and they get worse and worse until they are just terrible. This makes most of our patients get well very fast."

"I see," said Anne. "I feel well already. Thank you very much."

"Shall I give you Pill Number Two to take along in case you're not quite well?"

"No, thank you," said Anne politely. "I'd rather remember just the very best taste."

Mr. Drake was waiting for them in the outer room, and in another moment they were again on the way to the ball game.

6. The Bigger League

THEY walked only a few blocks when they came to a large ball field, with players already on it and a lot of children sitting on benches cheering their grandfathers.

Fortunately, just as they arrived, some of the children with schoolbooks under their arms got up and went racing away. This left plenty of room for Anne and Rickie and Mr. Drake.

It looked like an ordinary game, except that most of the players had white hair showing beneath their caps, and one of the coaches, who didn't wear a cap, was bald and shiny on top.

Two men were on bases, and the scoreboard showed it was the seventh inning, with the score tied at 3-3. The batter lunged at the ball, and missed.

"Strike one!" called the Umpire.

The batter took a good swing at the next one, and hit it hard. Rickie could see it would go over the left fielder's head. But neither the batter nor the runners were starting. Rickie bounced up, the way he did at home on a good hit.

"Run!" he shouted. "You can make home on it!"

The folks around just looked at him. The ball sailed

well over the fielder's head, as Rickie expected, and rolled to the edge of the field. But neither runner budged.

"You're out!" shouted the Umpire.

The batter grinned, walked over to the bench, and the other players patted him on the back as he sat down.

"How come he's out?" asked Rickie. "That was a safe hit!"

"Our rules are a little different," explained Mr. Drake. "We think that when a batter has the skill and strength to make a clean hit, he shouldn't have to run, too. He should get a reward, like being called out and allowed to go and sit down for a while."

"That's much more restful," said Anne. "I like that."

"But how do you get runs and win a game?"

"I forgot to tell you," said Mr. Drake. "In Upside-Down Town the team with the fewest runs wins."

The next batter took two strikes, and then hit a high fly that a fielder caught easily. The Umpire said nothing, and the man kept on batting.

"Balls stopped in the infield, fouls, and hits that are caught don't count anything," explained Mr. Drake. "You have to keep on batting until you get a hit and are out, or else —"

"Strike him on!" yelled a boy in front of them. "Strike him on, Grandpa!"

The next ball was a clean strike.

"Strike three!" shouted the Umpire. "Take your base."

The man flung down his bat angrily and trotted off to first base. The other two runners advanced.

"You see, if they get three strikes on you, then

you've got to run as a penalty," said Mr. Drake. "Now is when it gets exciting. The bases are loaded, and the Antiques have a poor batter up!"

He was a poor batter. After an infield tap and a few fouls, the pitcher got over his third strike. The crowd rose to their feet and cheered as the run was forced in.

"The Antiques are leading the Bigger League," said Mr. Drake, "but they're going to get licked today! This is great!"

Another run was forced in before a home run put the side out. Rickie was getting the hang of the new rules, and cheered with the rest when the Sixties went out in order, with three clean hits.

"I want to go shopping now," said Anne.

"I like this," said Rickie. "Let's stay for another inning."

"You mean, outing," said Mr. Drake. "In Upside-Down Town we think it's more sensible to call a thing where each team makes three outs an outing."

"Outing, then," agreed Rickie. "Besides, there's no use going shopping because we haven't any money."

"You really have no money?" said Mr. Drake. "Then you must go shopping at once. Come, I'll show you The Unstore."

7. School

ON the way to the shopping center they saw a great
big playground with a small building on one side.

"Is that a school?" asked Anne.

"Yes," said Mr. Drake, "that's the Upside-Down
Town School."

"Could we see it? Maybe it's different."

"Of course you can visit it," said Mr. Drake. "We
have plenty of time."

"But it won't do any good today," said Rickie. "I
just remembered; it's Saturday."

"So it is," said Mr. Drake. "So school is in session
right now. That's why some children left the ball game
before it was quite over."

"You mean, in Upside-Down Town the children
have to go to school on holidays, too?"

"Well, I wouldn't say 'have to,'" said Mr. Drake, "and I wouldn't say 'too.' The fact is, only the very good children are allowed to go to school at all, and here we hold school only on holidays. The other days children are so busy and so happy doing the work grownups do in other places that they haven't time for school. Anyway, they learn such a lot doing the grownup jobs that they don't need much special schooling."

By this time they had crossed the street and were entering the school building. They noticed big bars on the doors.

"Those bars are needed to keep children who aren't supposed to come from breaking in," observed Mr. Drake.

There was a long corridor with doors to classrooms on either side. They entered the first classroom.

At first it looked like almost any classroom, with about twenty desks for the children arranged in rows, a big desk for the teacher up front, and green chalkboards on the two sides of the room that didn't have windows. Then they noticed that on each desk was a big red apple, and the teacher was a man, a ruddy, rather fat man with a white beard.

"Looks just like Santa Claus," whispered Anne.

"Now that machines make so many of the toys,"

Rickie observed, "maybe Santa teaches school in Upside-Down Town in his spare time."

By this time the teacher had risen and was coming toward them.

"I see we have visitors," he said in a jolly voice. "I'm Professor Claus. What can we show you about the fine school we have here?"

"We don't mean to interrupt," said Rickie politely. "We just thought school might be different in Upside-Down Town, and we would like to see it."

"That's just fine," said Professor Claus. "We think we do have some new ideas in education here, and a very happy school."

"The pupils must like you," said Anne shyly. "You're going to have an awful lot of apples at recess time."

"Oh, those!" Professor Claus chuckled. "I've just given those apples to the pupils. In Upside-Down Town the teachers usually give presents to the pupils. It makes them cheerful, and nothing helps learning more than being well fed and liking the teacher. So today it was apples."

"Do you teach the same way we do?" asked Rickie. "Everything else seems so different here."

"I suppose we do approach things a different way sometimes," said Professor Claus. "Take History, for example. I imagine your teachers start away back somewhere, and then come around to the present?"

"Why, yes," said Rickie. "How else could you teach History?"

"Just the opposite, of course. We start where we are, here in Upside-Down Town, and then try to find out how we came here, and what happened before that, and so on back to Columbus discovering America, and why he ever wanted to do that, and what things were like in Europe where he came from."

"You mean, you teach History backwards?"

"We think it's the sensible way. On what other journey do you start out from where you've never been in order to get to where you are now? That's the silly way History is usually taught. Besides, that way there's no surprise. Everybody knows how it is going to come out."

Anne held both her hands to her ears.

"Stop, please, stop!" she said. "I'm too young to have History, and you are getting me all mixed up. Don't you teach some simple things, maybe different from what we learn in school?"

"Well," said Professor Claus, "today we have courses in elementary and advanced forgetting."

8. Elementary Forgetting

"FORGETTING?" asked Anne. "But I thought schools were for learning."

"That's what most people think," said Professor Claus. "But it leaves out a very important part of a sound education. As you get older you will find that the worst troubles in the world come, not from lack of knowledge, but from things people are unable to forget. Think how few squabbles there would be if people could forget their grudges, and the mean remarks other people make about them. Or better still, forget to make the mean remarks. Let's see, now; what's your name?"

"I'm Anne."

"Well, Anne, those nice green chalkboards against the wall aren't much use by themselves. What makes them useful?"

Anne noticed in the trough below them big sticks of white and red and yellow chalk.

"I know!" she said. "The chalk."

"True, chalk does help to make a chalkboard useful, but that is not enough. What else do you see?"

Anne looked and looked. Rickie looked too, and finally he said, "I think I know!"

"Wait a bit. I want Anne to find it for herself."

At last Anne said, "Erasers?"

"Right!" chuckled Professor Claus. "What good would a chalkboard be without a way to forget? So we do have erasers for chalkboards, but not yet for minds."

"My mind isn't full yet," broke in Rickie, "and maybe you could stick more in without erasing anything."

"Yes, but what's there now may be a big nuisance to you unless you learn to forget."

"I don't quite see how."

"Let's see, what's your name?"

"I'm Rickie."

"Well, Rickie, do you roller-skate?"

"Some. But once I hurt myself, so I'm careful now."

"See? If you could forget your falls, and just strike right out, what a fine skater you would be! If we could all forget our mistakes, what fine people we would be. But we have never learned forgetting."

"I can see now how important it is," said Anne. "So we oughtn't be keeping you from teaching your class. Can't we just listen?"

"Maybe that's the best way," said Professor Claus. He turned to the class.

"John, how are you coming along with forgetting to make faces at people?"

"Why, I didn't even think of making faces all last week except once, and that time I managed to forget it when the face was half made."

"That's splendid, John. Now next week I imagine you will forget it entirely, and I can give you a perfect zero. Now, Dorothy?"

A very plump girl in the third row stood up beside her desk.

"Dorothy, did you forget to eat candy between meals last week?"

"I did," said Dorothy proudly. "I forgot it completely all week long."

"What do the bathroom scales say?"

"I lost half a pound."

"Children, you see how helpful forgetting is? Dorothy gets a perfect zero this week. Now let us have the class exercise on Seven."

Together, the class repeated:

"*We have forgotten that seven and five are eleven, because they aren't. We have forgotten that seven and five are thirteen, because they aren't.*"

"The Seven's," explained Professor Claus, "are usually a great nuisance to children. They remember the wrong answers. So we are trying an experiment. If we can only forget the most likely wrong. answers, there will be nothing left but the right answer."

"I'm all mixed up again," complained Anne.

"This one may not work," admitted Professor Claus.

"We do better in simpler things like getting children to forget to talk in church and to forget to cross the street when the light is red."

"What is the course in advanced forgetting like?" asked Rickie.

"Ah, a good question. Why don't you go and see?"

"All right. Where is it?"

Professor Claus stroked his long white beard again, and then slowly shook his head.

"I'm so sorry. I teach the course myself, but I can't quite remember when or where."

9. The Unstore

AFTER shaking hands with Professor Claus and thanking him, Rickie and Anne hurried off with Mr. Drake to the shopping center.

"You do your shopping in that big building," said Mr. Drake. "We're very proud of The Unstore."

"The what?" asked Anne.

"The Unstore. It's sort of like an ordinary store, only we name it better. You see, in your stores they don't really want to store things; they want to get rid of them. So we call ours The Unstore, because we unstore things as fast as we can."

The children crossed the street and went into The Unstore. Mr. Drake went back to the Hotel to tell the clerk where they were in case the train was ready.

It looked like any big department store, with counters loaded with goods of every sort, and the usual signs here and there, like:

```
*  *  VISIT OUR BASEMENT FOR THE LOWEST VALUES  *
    *  *  BUY THE SMALL ECONOMY SIZE  *  *
        *  *  ASK FOR MISS INFORMATION  *  *
```

"I guess you want to go see the dolls," said Rickie.

"I don't, either," said Anne. "I've got a million dolls. I want a gold thimble, like Mommie's."

Thimbles were on the third aisle, to the left, said Miss Information when they asked her. But on the way to the third aisle they passed a rack full of baseball bats, yellow and brown and shiny and all sizes.

"Gee, I wish I had that medium-sized one!" said Rickie. "I bet I could hit a home run every time! But we haven't got any money."

"Excuse me," said a clerk, a boy just older than Rickie. "Did I understand that you could use a nice baseball bat? These are made by hand, with special care. Just feel the balance in this one. We'll be glad to unstore it for you."

Rickie pushed the bat away.

"I'd like it a lot," he said, "but I haven't any money."

"Money?" said the clerk, looking confused. "The customer doesn't need money. In The Unstore we pay you for taking things away, if you really want them. That bat, for instance. I can give you — yes, here's the Gift Tag — I can give you a dollar and a half to take that one."

"You mean, you pay us to take things?"

"Of course," said the clerk. "In Upside-Down Town, we all know that the greatest fun in life is in making nice things, or growing good things. Now this man who made your baseball bat, he loves to shape bats. Only there's no use in his making more bats until we get rid of these. So he pays us to dispose of his bats,

56

and we pay our customers to take them. Everybody is pleased."

"But if he has to pay to get rid of his bats, what does he live on?"

"If he needs shoes or bread or something, he just comes to The Unstore and we pay him to take away a pair of shoes or a loaf of bread. That makes some shoemaker and some baker happy, too. And it gives the batmaker the money to pay us to get rid of some of his bats."

Rickie thought this over for a moment.

"Well," he said, "what's to keep a lazy fellow from just getting all he needs and not working at all?"

"He could do that in your town, too," said the clerk. "Only first he'd have to steal something or punch somebody in the nose. Then you'd give him food and shelter and clothes and call it punishment. Here we know that not doing something useful is heavy punishment, and most people can't stand it very long."

"Rickie," said Anne, "stop objecting, and just take the bat and the money, so I can get my thimble."

The clerk held out the lovely baseball bat, a paper dollar, and two shiny quarters. Rickie took them.

"Thank you very much," said the clerk. "As soon as you use up that bat, be sure to come again."

10. The Flashdark

AFTER Rickie got his baseball bat so easily, Anne lost no time in rushing over to the third aisle in The Unstore and finding the thimbles, which in Upside-Down Town are worn only on thumbs and are called Thumbles. Anne found a Thumble that just fitted her. The girl was pleased, and gave her fifty cents for taking it, as she had rather expected.

"Now," said the clerk, "wouldn't you like to see our counter of Upside-Down Town specialties? Some of those items are not carried in ordinary stores."

"We'd like very much to see them," said Anne.

"Maybe we could get a present for Grandfather," added Rickie.

In a moment they reached the counter she pointed out. It didn't look like anything special until they examined the items in detail. One was a brown tube which Rickie picked up.

"That," said the young girl who was serving as clerk, "is our best Ulg. Ulg, of course, is *glue* spelled backwards, without the *e*. Ulg unfixes anything you want unfixed. Glue has its uses, but think of the many times when what you really need is Ulg — bottle caps that are on too tight, screws that won't come off, postage stamps you want to save, windows that stick, drawers that won't open. Ulg will unfix them for you."

"How nice," said Anne. " But have you anything for grandfathers?"

The clerk thought a moment.

"Yes, I have the very thing for you," she said, picking up a black cylinder with a glass end.

"That's just a flashlight," objected Anne. "I'm sure Grandfather has a flashlight."

"Ah, but this is quite different," said the clerk. "This is not a flashlight. It's a flashdark."

"What's a flashdark?"

"It's what the name says. Instead of a flash of light in the dark, it gives you a flash of dark in the light. If you are in a room with some people and for some reason you'd rather not be seen — a thing that happens to most of us — you just press the flashdark, and you're surrounded by darkness. If your grandfather wants to take a nap in the afternoon, he just presses the button and it's dark around him."

"We'll take it," said Anne. "It's just what Grandfather needs."

"I can offer you only one dollar for taking this flashdark," said the clerk. "It's very popular in Upside-Down Town, and we don't have to pay much to get rid of this item."

While she was putting a gay gift wrapping on the flashdark, the clerk from the Hotel rushed up.

"It's a good thing Mr. Drake told me you'd be here," Charlie said breathlessly. "Your train is ready. I've already sent your bag to the station."

Rickie held the bat under his arm, Anne grabbed the flashdark package in the hand that didn't have the Thumble, and they ran to the railway station.

"All aboard, ALL ABOARD!" the Conductor was shouting.

They had barely climbed aboard and taken their seats when the train began to move — backwards, of course. They were on the way to Lancaster and Grandfather's at last.

But as they pulled out of the station Rickie and Anne both leaned their noses against the window for a last look at the town where they had had so much fun.

They couldn't see anything.

"You're leaning on the flashdark!" said Anne.

"Oh, dear!" said Rickie.

He took his elbow off the window ledge where the flashdark package lay.

They had just time to see the sign on the station:

UPSIDE-DOWN
TOWN

getting smaller — and smaller —

UPSIDE-DOWN
TOWN

and smaller.

THE END